CAYMAN

CAYMAN

A Photographic Journey through the Islands

PHOTOGRAPHS BY

Amanda Lumry & Loren Wengerd

TEXT BY Laura Hurwitz

Vista Press

First edition published 2000 by Vista Press, LLC
PMB 741
15600 NE 8th #B-1
Bellevue, WA 98008
(425) 462-6144
info@vistapress.com
www.vistapress.com

ISBN 0-9662257-3-2

10   9   8   7   6   5   4   3   2

Printed and bound in Hong Kong by C&C Offset Printing Co., Ltd

A portion of the proceeds from this book are donated to the National Trust for the Cayman Islands. For more information about this organization, please contact:

The National Trust for the Cayman Islands
P.O. Box 31116 SMB
Grand Cayman, BWI
info@caymannationaltrust.org
www.caymannationaltrust.org

endpapers: close-up of a venus sea fan, by Loren Wengerd
dedication photo: blue chromes, by Mark Huck

We dedicate this book to those

who have treasured

and will always treasure

Cayman.

We could not have produced this book without the participation and support

of a number of Caymanians. Representing Seven Mile Beach to East End,

and George Town to Cayman Brac, they graciously and generously allowed

us into their homes, opened up their hearts, and shared their stories. Included

in this book are interviews with the following people: Gladwyn K. Bush,

Angela Bodden-Davis, Dorothy Ebanks, Hope Ebanks Glidden, Captain

Paul Hurlston, Joel Robert Johnson, Lindo McGowan, Hope Glidden

Stephenson, Earl Tomlinson, Reverend C. Russell Turner, Jr., Otto Watler,

Mrs. E. W. Whittaker, and Gabriel Zelaya.

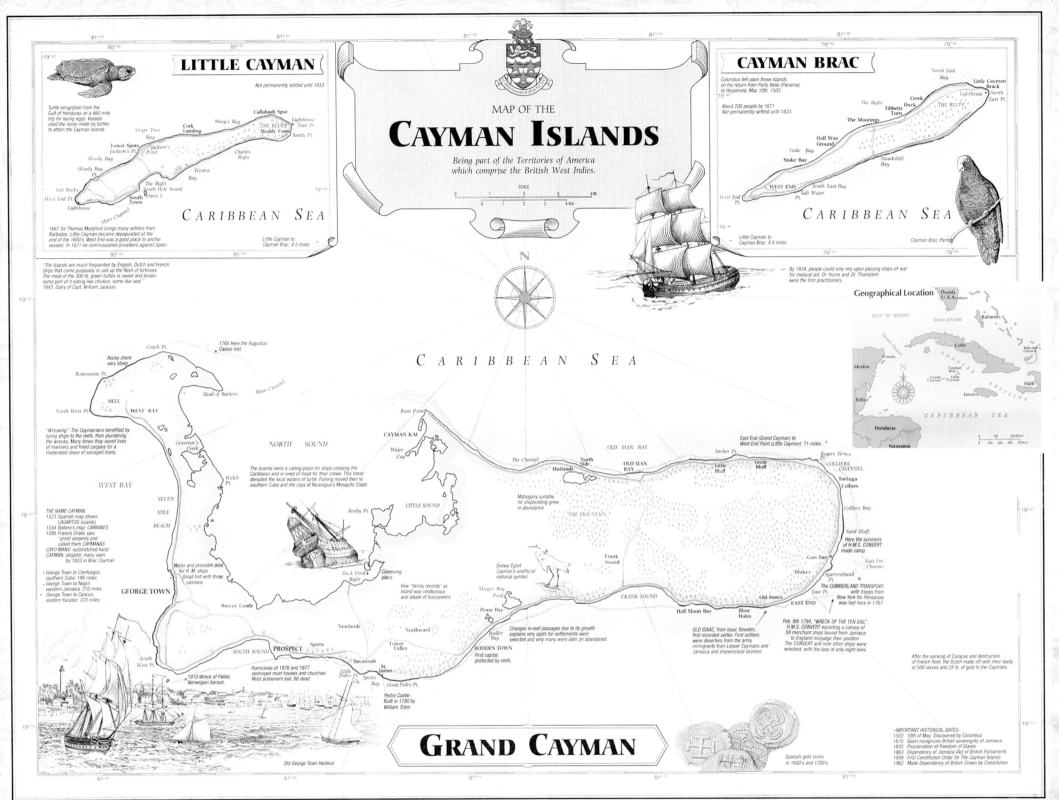

LITTLE CAYMAN

Not permanently settled until 1833

Turtle emigration from the Gulf of Honduras on a 460 mile trip for laying eggs. Vessels used the noose made by turtles to attain the Cayman Islands.

Callabash Spot
Mary's Bay
Cork Landing
Grape Tree Bay
THE BLUFF
Muddy Foots
Lighthouse
East Pt.
Sandy Pt.
Lower Spots
Jackson's Pt.
Jackson's Pond
Charles Bight
Bloody Bay
Bloody Bay Pt.
Wears Bay
Salt Rocks
West End Pt.
The Bight
South Hole Sound
South Town
Owen I.
Lighthouse
Main Channel

CARIBBEAN SEA

1667 Sir Thomas Modyford brings many settlers from Barbados. Little Cayman became depopulated at the end of the 1600's. West End was a good place to anchor vessels. In 1671 he commissioned privateers against Spain

Little Cayman to Cayman Brac: 4.5 miles

"The islands are much frequented by English, Dutch and French ships that come purposely to salt up the flesh of tortoises. The meat of the 300 lb. green turtles is sweet and tender, some part of it eating like chicken, some like veal." 1643. Diary of Capt. William Jackson.

MAP OF THE
Cayman Islands

Being part of the Territories of America which comprise the British West Indies.

SCALE

CAYMAN BRAC

Columbus fell upon these islands on his return from Porto Bello (Panama) to Hispaniola, May 10th, 1503.

About 200 people by 1671
Not permanently settled until 1833

North East Bay
Little Cayman Brac
North East Pt.
The Bight
Creek
Tibbetts Turn
Dock
Lighthouse
THE BLUFF
The Moorings
Half Way Ground
Stake Bay
Stake Bay
Hawksbill Bay
WEST END
South East Bay
West End Pt.
Salt Water

CARIBBEAN SEA

Little Cayman to Cayman Brac: 4.5 miles

By 1834, people could only rely upon passing ships-of-war for medical aid. Dr. Hume and Dr. Thompson were the first practitioners.

Cayman Brac Parrot

Geographical Location

GULF OF MEXICO
Florida U.S.A.
Miami
Bahamas
Mexico
Cuba
Cancun
Cayman Brac
Grand Cayman
Little Cayman
Haiti
Belize
GREATER ANTILLES
Jamaica
Honduras
CARIBBEAN SEA
Nicaragua

East End (Grand Cayman) to West End Point (Little Cayman): 71 miles

CARIBBEAN SEA

Conch Pt.
1765 Here the Augustus Caesar lost.
Rocky shore very steep
Boatswains Pt.
Head of Barkers
North West Pt.
HELL
WEST BAY
Main Channel
Rum Point
CAYMAN KAI
Water Cay

OLD MAN BAY
The Channel
North Side
Hutlands
OLD MAN BAY
Little Bluff
Great Bluff
Rogers Wreck
COLLIERS CHANNEL
Anchor Pt.
Tortuga
Colliers
Colliers Bay

NORTH SOUND

"Wrecking": The Caymanians benefited by luring ships to the reefs, then plundering the wrecks. Many times they saved lives of mariners and freed cargoes for a moderated share of salvaged booty.

Governor's Creek
WEST BAY
Welch Pt.
SEVEN MILE BEACH

The Islands were a calling place for ships crossing the Caribbean and in need of meat for their crews. This trend denuded the local waters of turtle. Fishing moved then to southern Cuba and the cays of Nicaragua's Mosquito Coast.

LITTLE SOUND
Booby Pt.
Sand Bluff
Here the survivors of H.M.S. CONVERT made camp.
THE MOUNTAIN

Mahogany suitable for shipbuilding grew in abundance.

THE NAME CAYMAN
1523 Spanish map shows LAGARTOS (lizards).
1554 Ballero's map: CAIMANES
1586 Francis Drake saw: "great serpents and called them CAYMANAS CAYO MANO outstretched hand CAYMAN: alligator, many seen by 1833 in Brac Cayman"

• George Town to Cienfuegos, southern Cuba: 198 miles
• George Town to Negril, western Jamaica: 210 miles
• George Town to Cancun, eastern Yucatan: 370 miles

GEORGE TOWN

Water and provision area for H.M. ships. Small fort with three cannons.

Duck Pond Bight
Careening place

Few "family records" as island was rendezvous and abode of buccaneers.

Snowy Egret Cayman's unofficial national symbol.
Frank Sound

Gun Bay
Blakes
Sparrowhawk Pt.
East End Channel
The CUMBERLAND TRANSPORT with troops from New York for Pensacola was lost here in 1767

Breezy Castle
Meagre Bay Pond
Pease Bay
FRANK SOUND
Old Issacs
EAST END
Half Moon Bay
Blow Holes

Newlands
Northward
Lower Valley
Nodder Bay

OLD ISAAC, from Isaac Bawden, first recorded settler. First settlers were deserters from the army; immigrants from Lesser Caymans and Jamaica and shipwrecked seamen.

Changes in reef passages due to its growth explains why spots for settlements were selected and why many were later on abandoned.

SOUTH SOUND
PROSPECT
Spotts
Savannah
St. James
Little Pedro Pt.
Spotts Bay
Great Pedro Pt.
BODDEN TOWN
First capital, protected by reefs.

South West Pt.

Feb. 8th 1794, "WRECK OF THE TEN SAIL". H.M.S. CONVERT escorting a convoy of 58 merchant ships bound from Jamaica to England misjudge their position. The CONVERT and nine other ships were wrecked, with the loss of only eight lives.

1910 Wreck of Pallas, Norwegian barque.

Hurricanes of 1876 and 1877 destroyed most houses and churches. Most schooners lost, 66 dead.

Pedro Castle: Built in 1780 by William Eden

Old George Town Harbour.

After the sacking of Curaçao and destruction of French fleet, the Dutch made off with their booty of 500 slaves and 28 lb. of gold to the Caymans.

GRAND CAYMAN

Spanish gold coins in 1600's and 1700's.

—IMPORTANT HISTORICAL DATES—
1503 10th of May: Discovered by Columbus
1670 Spain recognizes British sovereignty of Jamaica
1835 Proclamation of Freedom of Slaves
1863 Dependency of Jamaica (Act of British Parliament)
1959 First Constitution Order for The Cayman Islands
1962 Made Dependency of British Crown by Constitution

Art and design: Alejandro Rabazo (Toronto)

Contents

Foreword

One of my most precious memories of growing up in Cayman is one of working in the family shoestore with my aunts and cousins while on Christmas break from school. We knew everyone who came into the store, and it was a gathering spot for aunts, uncles, cousins, grandparents and friends. Each day someone brought in either a cooked ham or turkey, and we would enjoy eating it throughout the day. During the days leading up to Christmas most of the stores in town were open late. George Town was vibrant with people greeting each other and enjoying the novelty of the extended hours, while kids set off the "fire rackets" that were brought in especially for the holidays. Such a festive, warm and safe feeling surrounded the town. The gathering spots for friends and families and the time we had to share with each other gave us such a sense of community.

Even though the pace and appearance of Cayman have become more contemporary, our community spirit and decency still pervade the islands. It is the character of the people as well as the charm of our old homes and old streetscapes, the magnificence and beauty of our native flora and fauna that are a huge part of our appeal to more than a million visitors to our shores each year. The authors of *Cayman* have truly captured the people and places of the Cayman Islands that we treasure so deeply. These elements are so much a part of us, our spirit, our culture, and our way of life. And so, to provide for our future generations, it is clear that there must be a balance between development and the preservation of our natural and historic environments.

In 1987 a group of Caymanians and residents who were concerned with the impact of the islands' rapid growth on our natural and historic environments founded The National Trust for the Cayman Islands. Through research, documentation, acquisition, advocacy and education, the National Trust is working to raise awareness and appreciation of "things Caymanian". We are very grateful to Vista Press for donating part of the proceeds of *Cayman* to the National Trust for the Cayman Islands. As a non-government, non-profit organization we depend on this kind of support to achieve our mission: *to preserve natural environments and places of historic significance for present and future generations of the Cayman Islands.*

Cayman is a beautiful keepsake and is filled with outstanding photographs of Grand Cayman, Cayman Brac and Little Cayman. It highlights, through small biographies, the warmth, charm and diversity of the Caymanian people and shows the contemporary side of Cayman as well as insights into local traditions and culture. By purchasing this book you will support the Trust's commitment to the preservation of our past and the promise of our future. We hope you enjoy Cayman and that you too will come to treasure it.

Wendy Moore
EXECUTIVE DIRECTOR
NATIONAL TRUST FOR THE CAYMAN ISLANDS

Acknowledgments

We would like to thank the Lord for creating these beautiful islands and the opportunity to see our dreams come true once again.

Thank you Mother Hope and Pie for adopting us into your family. You taught us so much about Cayman and introduced us to so many of your friends.

We would like to thank the National Trust under the guidance of Wendy Moore for its role in preserving the Cayman Islands.

Thank you for all of your help, Grace.

Rufus--from visualization to realization, thanks for being there every step of the way.

We would like to thank Emily McGalliard for her hard work, design talent and limitless level of energy.

Thanks to Reid McNeal and Mark Huck for their underwater guidance and expertise.

We would like to express our gratitude to Andrew L. Guthrie at the Queen Elizabeth II Botanic Park for his identification of flora and fauna sprinkled throughout the book.

Thank you Gist and C&C Offset Printing Co. Ltd for their high quality color reproduction and printing.

We would like to thank Joni Bomstead, Scott Drum, Nanda Mehta and Maryan Regan for their continual support of our projects. Your invaluable advice and organizational skills are the reason we are able to do what we do.

To the Cayman Christmas Clan, this one is for you.

Amanda wishes to thank her parents, Rufus and Patricia, and her brothers, Worth and Chris, for their love.

Laura wants to thank Sam, Hannah, Jake, Rachel, Sarah, Eliza, and Mike for their love and support. And Claudia, you're the best (but you already know that).

Loren would like to thank his parents, Eli and Marcella, for their encouragement and support, and his siblings, who taught him to take things to the edge.

Strolling Seven Mile Beach

From the Wharf Restaurant to West Bay, there runs a long stretch of pristine sand known as Seven Mile Beach. Regarded by many to be the most beautiful beach in the world, it features elegant beachfront homes and hotels, graceful palm and casuarina trees, and fine ivory sand bordered by translucent turquoise waters. However, there is more to this beach than the beauty you'll find at the water's edge. Like a tiered cake, Seven Mile Beach consists of several layers, each uniquely delightful.

Bordering the street which parallels the beach (West Bay Road) are wonderful shops with a full spectrum of merchandise and services to offer. From superb five-star restaurants to casual fast-food places, from designer dress shops to T-shirt boutiques, and from stores that carry the finest imported jewelry and china to those that sell inexpensive souvenirs, this retail area encompasses both extremes and everything in between.

Once you cross over to the oceanfront, you can see the classic older hotels and condominiums, and those that are breathtakingly new. The architecture ranges from traditional Caymanian to ultra-modern glass and steel, but all of

these structures are oriented toward the beautiful waters of the Caribbean.

The beachside itself is the rarest jewel of all. The water's variations of hue, from palest green to turquoise to indigo, shift and move with the light. The ocean's surface can be turbulent, rolling, choppy, or smooth as polished glass. Offshore storms can cause the waves to crest and peak with almost symphonic drama. Seven Mile Beach is itself a nautical masterpiece. The waves have chiseled out the shoreline, smoothing out patches of craggy coral and refining and restoring precious sand.

As the beach faces west, you will be privy to the most spectacular sunsets you can possibly imagine. These sunsets provide the perfect inspiration for romantic beach walks, as any number of hand-holding couples can attest. Then after dusk, the moon rises, dancing along the water's edge. For early risers, this same seascape provides a crisp, inviting environment for a run or walk. Day or night, the moist, fine-grained sand embracing your toes and the gentle

rhythmic lapping of the water provide an unforgettable sensation.

Seven Mile Beach is the hub of Grand Cayman's tourist industry. Here, one never runs short of things to do. Parasailing, paddle boating, kayaking, jet skiing, snorkeling, scuba diving, whatever you might like to try, you can be certain it is available at one of the many water sport facilities on the beach. Or, if these diversions sound too ambitious, you can simply pull up a lounge chair and sit on the beach. Between the clarity and beauty of the waters, the softness of the sand, and the world-class hotels, condominiums, and restaurants, you could happily stay forever on this seven-mile stretch of pure paradise. 🐚

RIGHT: You don't have to be all grown up to enjoy the setting sun.
OPPOSITE ABOVE: Card sharks on the beach at the Cayman Reef Resort
OPPOSITE BELOW: Surf's up and school's out at the West Bay Public Beach.

"I remember thinking, never have I seen a
more beautiful color than this ocean."

Cayman resident of Brazilian origin

 Strolling Seven Mile Beach

Captain
Paul
Hurlston
retired

seaman

Captain Paul welcomes us into his dark, simply-furnished living room and motions for us to sit. "Excuse the appearance, but I'm a man living alone," he says, with more than a touch of sorrow in his voice. There are a few knick-knacks placed around the room in an effort to decorate, but it is apparent that the house lacks a feminine touch. During the course of our interview, Captain Paul tells us how his wife left him three years ago, and that he is still in love with her. While telling us this, he shows us a stack of love letters he had saved, dating back to 1959. He still clings doggedly to a fragment of hope that she'll come back to him, but a weariness and resignation seems to overshadow his faith in a marital reunion.

Captain Paul has a son and a daughter, but he only sees his son on occasion and doesn't see his daughter at all. "I'm not close to my daughter, unfortunately. She doesn't care to hear about the old days." He finds an enthusiastic audience in us, though, and proceeds to tell us about his past. He is one of ten children, six boys and four girls. One of his brothers and all four sisters are still alive. In 1941, his older brother was lost on a schooner during a hurricane. That event had caused him to wonder if there might not be an easier and safer way to make a living than from the sea, but on Cayman there were no real options. It was simple: Caymanian men, unless they farmed, found employment on boats. Captain Paul left Cayman in his early teens on a voyage to catch turtles off the coast of Nicaragua. He was a bit nervous, but excitement at the prospect of making money prevailed, and off he went. On this expedition, he earned the princely sum of 48 pounds. This new-found affluence had him hooked. He would spend the next four decades at sea. Rummaging around in a drawer, he unearths his first passport. Looking at his photograph, he points and laughs. "Look! You can see the mosquitoes on my face. They were the mark of living on Cayman."

What else could Captain Paul tell us about life on old Cayman? He smiles and says, "You know?

If I had to come up with a symbol for the Cayman Islands, it would be a woman. Those Cayman women, they held this place together." He tells us how the men would be gone at sea for months or even years at a time, leaving their wives to raise the children, run the farms and businesses, and in general keep things afloat until their husbands returned. Children, he said, attended school from the time they were seven to the time they were fourteen, at which time, "well, if they

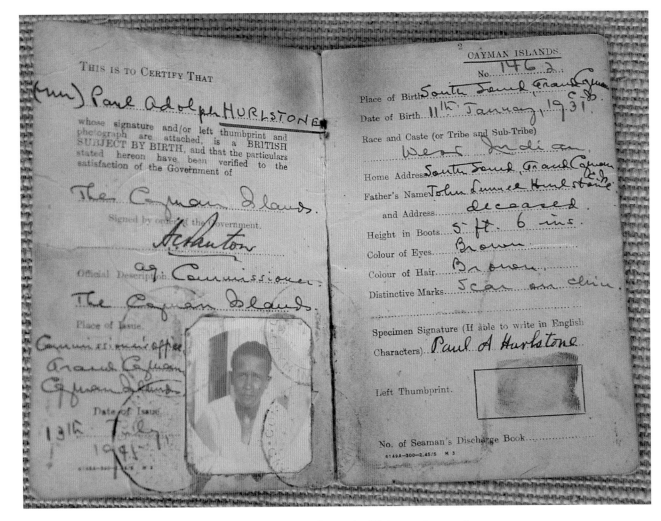

"Look! You can see the mosquitoes on my face. They were the mark of living on Cayman."

learned anything, fine, if not then they leave, anyway!" The Church was at the center of island life. Church suppers, prayer meetings, picnics—all social activities revolved around a spiritual center. Captain Paul loved the simplicity of island life. Even so, there were difficult times, too, such as the rainy seasons of his boyhood, when the mosquitoes got so bad that you'd be forced to get a smoke-pot, fill it with a special type of noxious-smelling wood called smoke wood, or dried cow dung (your choice), then light it at the door of your house to smoke the pests away. In addition to lighting the smoke-pot, you'd have to close up all the windows and doors in an effort to keep the smell of the smoke-pot outside. "It got so that you didn't know what was worse, the smell or the mosquitoes." Captain Paul tells us stories about cattle in the field choking to death when swarmed by the insects, and about how you had to carry a mosquito brush with you at all times during the rainy season to keep the mosquitoes away. Things got better, he says, when a man named Dr. Giglioli came to Cayman in 1964 to direct the Mosquito Research and Control Unit, which initiated a pesticide blitz that dramatically reduced the number of mosquitoes on the island.

Captain Paul, like many older Caymanians, misses the old days. He does, however, see the benefit of today's better health care and schooling. He also acknowledges that financially, Cayman is stronger than ever. He knows that he can't turn back the clock, and if he could, he's not sure that he'd want to, except, perhaps, to reunite with his wife. But he cares passionately about a small link to the past. When he was a boy, the small inlet on the South Shore known as Smith's Cove was called Smith's Barcadere. The name changed, he feels,

because tourists thought it odd, or they had trouble pronouncing it. Captain Paul wants the original name reinstated. "That's all I ask for," he says. "How can you change a name like that? It isn't right. I want that small part of old Cayman back."

Strolling Seven Mile Beach

ABOVE: An idyllic swing at the Villas of the Galleon

OPPOSITE RIGHT: Parasailing is the best way to get a bird's eye view of Cayman.

OPPOSITE LEFT ABOVE: The net is up at Treasure Island.

ABOVE: Come out and play! The sea is open at the Radisson.

OPPOSITE TOP: Looking west from Crescent Point

OPPOSITE BELOW: Fishing early in the morning

Sea crab

Dorothy
Ebanks
"Dodie"
returned
native &
committed
volunteer

"In spite of the changes to Cayman, it is still the most wonderful place in the world. Nowhere on earth can compare to Cayman."

Dramatic? Perhaps. But these words come from a woman who had to make a choice—a long life in England, or a significantly shorter life in her beloved Cayman. Dodie Ebanks chose Cayman.

Dodie is no stranger to adversity. Much of her face, including one eye and her nose, have been destroyed by a skin condition which is a result of exposure to the ultraviolet rays of the sun. As anyone who has visited Cayman can tell you, the sun here is usually out, and it is quite intense. Dodie was born on Cayman and spent her childhood here, gradually becoming more and more ill until she reached a point where virtually all her time was spent in the hospital. At the age of fifteen, when her condition seemed irreversible and most certainly terminal, her doctor advised her to go to a research hospital in England where, with luck, doctors could help her and in doing so help others with a similar condition. Instead, doctors at the English hospital determined the cause of Dodie's illness and treated her by keeping her out of the sun. While still a patient, she met the man who would become her husband, and she stayed in England for the next twenty-five years. During this time, Dodie raised a son and a daughter and led a full life, but she always remained aware of an emptiness in her heart. She realized she missed Cayman. When her marriage dissolved and her children were grown, Dodie felt she had to make a choice. She knew that returning home would eventually kill her, and she knew that her daughter, who needed regular dialysis which was not available in Cayman, would not be able to come with her. She had all but decided to stay in England when her daughter, Ruth, and son, Mark, encouraged her to leave. "Ever since I can remember, you have always been homesick for Cayman," Ruth told her. "Go. I'll be fine."

So, Dodie returned to Cayman, facing the grim prognosis that she would survive for maybe five years at best. Shortly after her arrival on Cayman, her daughter Ruth died in England. Dodie's only

Sea grapes

regret was that she could not be with Ruth during this time, although she feels that Ruth became joyfully independent as a result of being allowed to be on her own. But looking back—and Dodie has had thirteen years on Cayman to look back over—she feels she made the right choice. "I know I'll probably die soon," Dodie says, without a trace of self-pity. "But I love my island. This is home."

Dodie's sense of humor is transcendent. She tells a story about waiting out a strong hurricane with a group of friends in a condo directly on Seven Mile Beach, and how the young daughter of one of her friends, when told that the windows should be taped to prevent them from breaking, took the surgical tape Dodie needed for her prosthetic eye and taped all the windows. "I had to go without my eye for a week, until the supply ships came in," Dodie tells us, doubled over with laughter.

In a more serious mood, she reflects on what Cayman has lost over the past decades—the ties to family, the numerous traditions such as hat-making that won't be passed down to subsequent generations, and the loss of many of the trees, most notably the naseberry, cocoa plum, and the mango, to both storms and construction. She clearly relishes talking about her favorite Caymanian food, from fish run-downs, salt beef and beans, to fresh seafood and the rich heavy cakes. She notes the change in the taste of turtle meat, saying that turtles caught in the wild had a superior taste to turtles cultivated at the turtle farm. She's optimistic, though, seeing much positive change, including better, readily available medical care and greater educational opportunities for island children. Whenever she gets nostalgic and wishes for the old days, she looks around and says, "Wait. This is still my island."

Dodie Ebanks inspired us. Rarely do people have to make a choice such as hers, and her decision to return home speaks profoundly about both her courage and the pull of these beautiful Cayman Islands.

"Each person here is his brother's keeper."

resident for the past decade

ABOVE: Mopeds lined up waiting to explore the island

TOP LEFT: Treasure Island

BOTTOM LEFT: Lounge chairs waiting for occupants in front of the Westin Casuarina Resort

ABOVE: The Hyatt Regency's elegant pool looks cool and inviting.

TOP: Sea pines grace the beachside view of the Sovereign.

LEFT: A gracious turret draped with tropical flowers beckons visitors at the Coralstone Club.

RIGHT: A parasailer's view along Seven Mile Beach

BELOW: Looking south toward George Town, a Carnival cruise ship comes in. The wreck of the Cali is in the forground.

BOTTOM: Ready to relax beachside at The Pinnacle

OPPOSITE: Feed the Tarpon at the Wharf.

Strolling Seven Mile Beach

Strolling Seven Mile Beach

"Welcome to my little
slice of paradise."

condo owner

Silver thatch palm, the islands' national
tree

Angela
Bodden
Davis
mother &
banking
professional

In the shade of a palm tree near West Bay's public beach, Angela Bodden Davis sits with her one-year-old daughter Daniella while she watches her six-year-old son Gavin play happily in the shallow water.

Like most Caymanians, Angela speaks quite fondly of the island, and hopes that her children will continue to live here when they grow up. Most of Angela's family resides in the United States and Jamaica. Angela has visited the States several times, and she does love to travel, but she points out that "when I'm away, I find myself getting homesick quite a bit." Cayman's small-town feeling serves as a solid foundation, while tourists come and go. "Even if we don't recognize the name, once we see the face, we definitely recognize a fellow Caymanian. You just feel safe here. We have a lot of respect for each other. The people here are warm and friendly."

Grand Cayman anole

ABOVE: Only a small piece of land stretches between the oceanside and harborside.

OPPOSITE: A father and daughter find the perfect way to spend an afternoon together.

FOLLOWING PAGE: Farewell, Cayman. A cruise ship departs.

Diving Deep

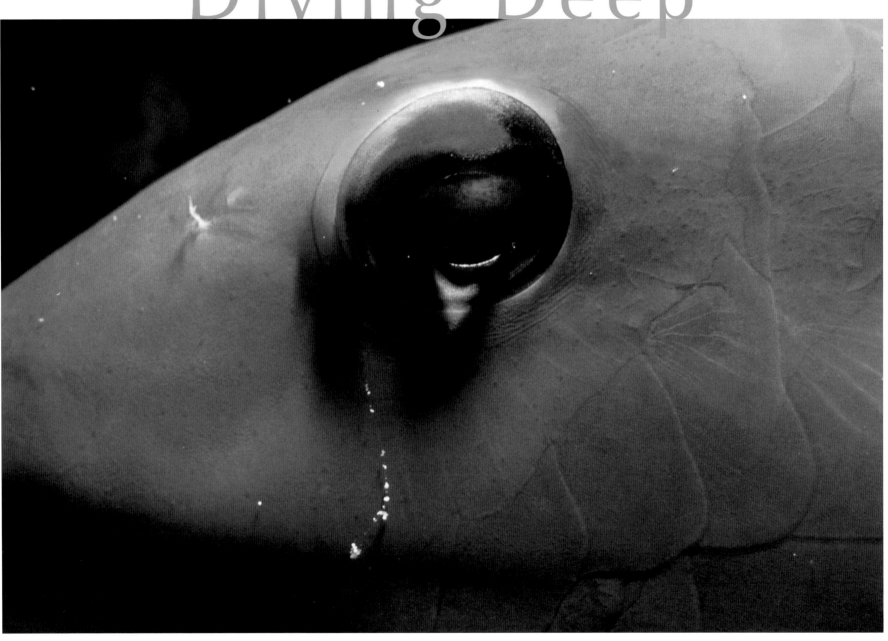

*I*magine mountains, some over one thousand feet high, submerged under a warm Caribbean sea. That is, in fact, what the Cayman Islands are: the peaks of an underwater mountain range, surrounded by incomparably beautiful coral reefs which end as a wall, dropping sharply away to the ocean floor a thousand feet below. This environment is home to a plethora of fascinating marine creatures, from big to small, fixed to fast-moving. You can swim with a school of blue tang or examine the coral growing on the hull of a sunken ship. Hovering slightly above the sandy bottom or beside the precipitous one thousand foot drop-off, divers are amazed by the enormously rich assortment of sea life, including turtles, reef sharks, tarpon, grouper, and moray eels. Also awe-inspiring are the spectacular giant sponges and dramatic cliffs, as well as the unique grottos and mysterious caves.

For those certified to scuba dive, the three islands offer hundreds of fantastic dive sites. Divers can explore walls, coral gardens, caves, canyons, gullies, and wrecks, and any number of skilled dive operators are ready and

ABOVE: Air tanks are stacked and ready to use.

TOP: Eden Rock Diving Center

OPPOSITE: Photographed at Royal Palms Ledge, the rough fileclam inhabits narrow cracks and crevices, and swims by repeatedly snapping its valves open and shut.

PREVIOUS PAGE: Diver hovering over barrel sponges

CHAPTER OPENER: Blue parrot fish produce quite a bit of the sand, often colorful, found on the beach and ocean floor. At night they secrete a protective membrane or sac around their bodies.

willing to take divers out. For the most adventurous, night dives provide a different kind of Cayman night life. Using flashlights, night divers illuminate the vibrant colors of the fish and coral immediately surrounding them. Divers can become easily disoriented underwater in the dark, so they must watch their bubbles to determine which way is up. For those who want to take underwater photographs, the clarity of the water around Grand Cayman, Cayman Brac, and Little Cayman is incomparable, offering visibility at up to 150 feet. The most dedicated divers have been known to frequent Little Cayman, the location of Bloody Bay Wall, considered one of the best dive sites in the world.

Another option, for those not certified to dive but seeking a deep water adventure, is the Atlantis Submarine trip. This vessel travels one hundred feet under the surface of the water in George Town harbor and allows its passengers to view marine life from the comfort of an air-conditioned sub. Atlantis also features the Deep Explorer, a smaller submersible that holds two passengers and the pilot, and descends to a depth of one thousand feet down the Cayman Wall. The sponges, coral, and the 150-foot "haystacks," which are actually underwater limestone blocks, can be viewed up close from this unique research vessel.

The Stingray City experience offers scuba divers the opportunity to swim with these elegant creatures in twelve feet

RIGHT: Peterson cleaning shrimp form a symbiotic arrangement with fish by hitching a ride and cleaning the parasites and other bothersome organisms off the fish. Often they are found near corkscrew anemones.

BELOW: As photographed here at Waldo's Reef, divers are more likely to see a Caribbean reef squid at night. These creatures change color or lighten or darken dramatically. To swim slowly it uses the thin fin on the sides of its body, while a jet of water propels the squid more rapidly, similar to the movement of an octopus.

OPPOSITE: Just beyond the reef a large school of blue chromes search for small creatures and algae floating through the water.

of water (Stingray City has been dubbed "the Best Twelve-Foot Dive in the World"). Snorkelers can stand waist-deep on a sandbar adjacent to Stingray City, while these docile creatures swim gracefully around them.

A popular Cayman saying warns that if you don't investigate the underwater world around Cayman, you've missed seventy-five percent of the Islands. Under the surface of the azure sea lies a vast, mysterious realm, teeming with life and color. Whether you grab your snorkel, don a wet suit and air tank, or book a submarine tour, just be certain you get down there and explore.

ABOVE: Normally scared off by an approaching diver, a feeding green sea turtle is very shy and usually swims away deceptively quickly. In this case, the turtle has failed to notice its observer while eating a tasty sponge.

RIGHT: Contrary to what you see in the movies, the timid reef shark usually keeps its distance from divers, and is rarely seen, as it spots humans well before being spotted.

OPPOSITE: Divers and fish at Aquarium South. Some popular dive sites are great for interacting with the fish. These fish, always looking for a handout, will actually seek out divers who are willing to stop and play for a while.

"Buoyancy control is key to approaching subjects in the water without scaring them off. If you have driven away the creature by excessive movement, you have lost your opportunity to be creative. This is where photography becomes art, not just snapshots."

underwater photography instructor

TOP: Turtle and diver, swimming side by side.

MIDDLE: A stingray skates gracefully along the ocean floor.

BOTTOM: Snorkelers feeding an eel.

OPPOSITE: A moray eel peeking out from its hiding spot.

ABOVE: A vivid strawberry sponge amidst rope sponges
RIGHT: Symmetrical brain coral
OPPOSITE: A fairy basslet, also known as a "royal gramma",
rests suspended at Sheer Wall, Little Cayman. A diver may
see this two-inch fish swimming upside-down near the
ceiling of a cave or ledge.

45

Diving Deep

ABOVE: Christmas tree worms, mostly less than one and a half inches tall, come in a variety of colors, usually in darker tones. They pull back into their tubes very quickly to protect themselves from predators, and emerge again very slowly.

LEFT: Horse-eye jacks and tarpon (larger fish) photographed at Bonnie's Arch. These fish rarely school together, but both kinds will occasionally allow divers to swim very close.

ABOVE: A beautiful, shy eagle ray glides effortlessly through the water much like an eagle soaring through the air. These creatures have been seen jumping up out of the water six to eight feet in the air, even from an almost stationary position.

OPPOSITE LEFT: The violet variety of social feather dusters swaying gently in the current.

OPPOSITE RIGHT: Multiple appendages surround the mouth of these anemones. Using stinging nematocysts in their tentacles, they pull their food to the center where they can slowly digest, taking as long as fourteen to sixteen hours. Most often a small anemone crab and tiny shrimp inhabit an anemone, taking advantage of the undigested food.

"The greatest joy in the water is
that feeling of weightlessness.
Anything that nature gives you
beyond that is a bonus."

diving instructor

This coney, in its golden phase, is an uncommon sight. Divers more often observe a reddish or brownish coloration on this six- to ten-inch fish.

A brown spotted eel at West Wall. These mean looking animals get a bad rap because their mouths, which are full of sharp teeth angled in to hold their prey, are always opening and closing, giving the impression that they want to bite you. In fact, they are very shy and often retract, as in the case of the moray eel, into the hole in which they are temporarily residing.

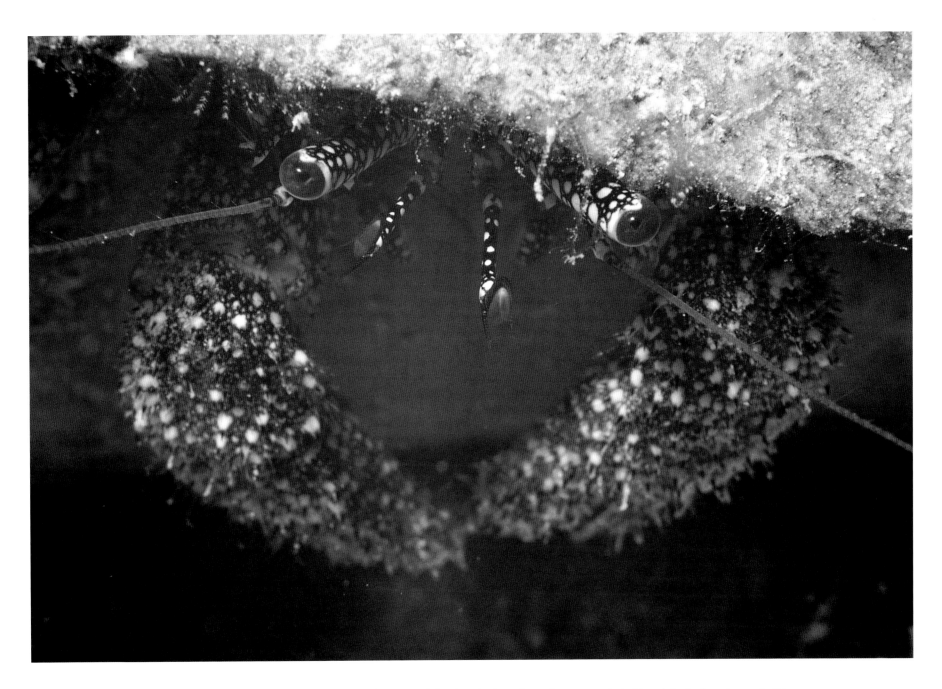

ABOVE: The small hermit crab will inhabit a vacated shell or the shell of an animal that has died. As the crab outgrows its habitat, it looks for a larger shell to occupy.

OPPOSITE: Taken at Hammerhead Hole, the uncommon sight of a gaudy clown crab.

Diving Deep

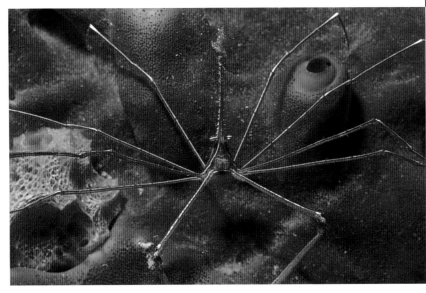

Diving Deep

BELOW: Preparing the Deep Explorer for an underwater adventure.

RIGHT: Stalked crinoid taken at a depth of one thousand feet from the Deep Explorer.

OPPOSITE

TOP: A diamond blemmy, a fish found all over the reef, rests in a great sea anemone.

MIDDLE: Flamingo tongue inching up a branch of coral.

BELOW: Most people mistake the arrow crab for a spider. Usually found near or on sponges, they can be seen at night moving to the top of sponges to feed on things that the sponge is siphoning through it.

Living Life Cayman Style

eel the gentle tempo of pure relaxation, best experienced floating on a raft surrounded by warm, azure Caribbean waters, or perhaps lying on a hammock beneath the benevolent shade of a palm tree while tropical breezes cool your skin. Feel your pulse race as you skim along the water's surface on the back of a wave-runner or as you dance on the beach at midnight to a calypso band. On these islands offering both utter tranquility and ultimate thrills, residents assume the islands' quintessential back-beat pace. Caymanians move as fast or as slowly as the waves on the shore.

Life in Cayman echoes this rhythm. Bankers here conduct business much as they do elsewhere, but you might not even realize that work is being done because of the friendly banter and casual tropical attire of the customers. On Sunday morning, cars flood into church parking lots and people emerge in their Sunday best, ready to slow down, hear God's Word, and greet each other after a busy week.

In a restaurant, we overheard a conversation between two businessmen, one American, the other Caymanian. The Caymanian told the American to meet him at the bank at

Plumeria, or frangipani, from the Botanic Park, was once commonly known as a "graveyard tree."

one o'clock. "One o'clock real time, or one o'clock Cayman?" the American responded, with a laugh. Time has a flexible and forgiving quality here.

Perhaps the reason for this is that the people of Cayman, no matter how busy they might be, make you feel as if they have all the time in the world. Drivers honk their horns, not to signal their impatience, but as a way of saying hello, or to signal you that they are graciously allowing your car to slip in front when there is traffic. While ringing up your order, the cashier in the drugstore chats with a friend who has stopped by. A tour of the island's hamlets reveals many front doors, open wide, to embrace both air in motion and any visitors who might happen by. Open doors, open hearts—no one stays a stranger on Cayman.

Whether you've been ferried in from a cruise ship for a day in George Town, or you're staying for a week in a luxury hotel on Seven Mile Beach, savor your time. Feast on the food, from native dishes to haute cuisine. Watch the sun set, visit a historic building, scuba dive, or sip a cold drink from the comfort of your beach chair. Move fast, or move slow. But however long your stay, and whatever you choose to experience, learn from the Caymanians. Pause for a moment. Take a deep breath. Let the islands set the pace, and you will find yourself moving to the rhythm of the sea, which sets the fundamental pulse of life, Cayman style. 🐚

ABOVE: Laundry blowing in the ocean breeze on East End.

OPPOSITE: Trompe d'ouille facada on a house on East End.

CHAPTER OPENER: Mother hen and her brood on the move.

FACING CHAPTER OPENER: After school at the West Bay Public Beach, a young boy enjoys the effects of the previous night's storm.

Lindo
McGowan
& Gabriel
Zelaya
fishermen

In George Town, next to Don Foster's Dive Shop, five men ranging in age from about ten to sixty-five bring in their catch for the day. They head out around 6:00 A.M. and return by noon to clean and sell their forty or so pounds of parrotfish, which they can count on selling all in a day. Every few weeks, they venture out around sixty miles from the shore for three to four days to catch snapper, grouper, triggerfish, tuna, and mahi mahi. We watch as a steady stream of people dressed in business attire pick up tonight's supper. Gabriel Zelaya looks up from his work, long, bloody knife in hand. He smiles and asks, "Are you falling in love with this place yet?"

LEFT: An historical family home in downtown George Town.

RIGHT: This neo-traditional home has a great view of the water to the north.

BELOW: Windsurfer in South Sound sails by.

OPPOSITE: Traditional house in East End

Allamanda

"I wouldn't change a thing here. The rest of Cayman, it got so built up."

East End resident

Ruellia

ABOVE: Decorated tombs overlook a sweep of ocean on the north side.

LEFT: Powell's Museum in West Bay is located at the entrance of the picturesque street known as Boggy Sand Road.

Otto
Watler
farmer,
beekeeper, &
conservationist

Simply put, Otto Watler is a farmer. With the help of his son, Bruce, and three workers from Jamaica, he grows mangoes, raises cattle, and keeps bees, in addition to spending much of his time regenerating the numbers of the native Caymanian parrot. His family has been farming Lower Valley for several generations. Through his life's work he has developed a broad understanding of, and deep respect for, the island's ecology.

A self-educated conservationist, Otto has found a comfortable compromise between two bitterly opposing sides on the subject of parrots. Generally, mango growers hate the sight of the indigenous Cayman parrot, which eats big chunks out of perfectly ripe fruit, and thus out of the growers' profits. Despite the fact that he owns one of the largest mango groves on Cayman, Otto asserts that he is "on the parrot's side." For ten years he has appointed himself the parrots' advocate by attempting to breed them in captivity and then release them before they become the least bit domesticated. He first built small cages only to discover that "if you take something free as a bird and put it in captivity, it will get stressed out." When some of the birds exhibited such odd behavior as pulling their feathers out, and when several males in one cage became extremely aggressive with one another, especially during mating season, Otto and his son built a huge labyrinth of cages, more like an aviary, to give them a more natural habitat.

By this point, in 1996 the government had placed the Cayman parrot on the endangered list. Due to the ban on hunting since that time, the parrots' numbers have risen from about 1,500 to more than 2,000, which of course takes its toll on mango growers. But considering the bigger picture, Otto maintains, "I own 140 to 150 mango trees on about ten acres, and I grow 14,000 pounds of mangoes each year. Two hundred and fifty pounds out of that are for the parrots. If I can't give back this much to nature, then something is wrong with me....I measure a man by how he can make the ecosystem better than how he found it." At the same time that he holds high standards for himself and his fellow humanity, he carries the highest regard for his homeland and its inhabitants. "I travel and keep up with the world, but I don't think there's another place in the world like this....True Caymanians are the most decent, God-fearing, intellectual people."

We drive down the road to the Lower Valley, where Otto's orchard is filled with rows of trees adorned

LEFT: Bees produced several hundred pounds of honey in this old sailfish base.
BELOW: Regarding the tourists from a bovine perspective on Otto Watler's cattle ranch.

with plump, ripe mangoes. The wake of damage caused by Hurricane Gilbert in '81 has left a permanently stumped pathway. This orchard, which his grandfather used for cattle grazing, was planted by Otto in 1976 and produced the first harvest in 1980, which was followed the next year by Gilbert's devastation. He confesses he feels quite sentimental about this area, where he used to walk behind his grandfather. Selling it, he says, would be like parting with his soul.

Otto's knowledge of the land only begins with his fruit (three varieties—Tommy Atkins, Kent, and Keith, which

"I grow 14,000 pounds of mangoes each year. Two hundred and fifty pounds out of that are for the parrots. If I can't give back this much to nature, then something is wrong with me." -Otto Watler

come into season in that order). With equal pleasure and intensity, he guides us through every kind of plant on the property, making sure to point out the doves and a black arni, which don't eat his mangoes. Cattle love the guinea grass and wild tamarind. The guinip blossom attracts bees for his honey operation. He breaks off a sample leaf of maiden plum, which contains a milky substance that smells like petroleum. One drop of that on your skin, and poison ivy will seem benign by comparison. A lone wild guava tree grows here and a wild key lime over there. Mounds of flint rock surface everywhere, hinting at the difficulty with which Otto has cultivated his land. Hit a piece of flint and watch the sparks fly. Silver thatch, the palm tree found all over the island and that everyone associates with the tropics, has a history as well. Caymanians used to twist three lines of string out of the flowering part of the tree, to fashion a rope strong enough to anchor their fish traps. A gourd tree bears some large, unlikely looking fruit, the shell of which Otto and his family would use as a cup after seasoning with lime juice. Sadly, most of the island's mahogany has succumbed to the boating industry, although cedar, he points out, still survives. Overhead a bat house built by fellow conservationist Lois Blumenthal, reminds him to tell us that bats are our friends. Just as he explains that they pass their food in four hours, spreading seeds everywhere, a rare sight suddenly materializes on a lone fig tree. A flock of Australian squawking parrots circle noisily

in perfect formation before landing together on the same tree. Apparently, a few pet birds escaped from their cage in their owner's garage and have been breeding and thriving out in the open ever since. Even the old base of a sailfish propped against a tree has a story to go with it. Not long ago, the boat became so heavy with honey from bees that had settled inside it, that it took four men to carry it out.

We make our way back to the house and Otto's wife Sybil shows us a commendation Otto received from Queen Elizabeth in 1995 for his "service in the field of conservation," as well as a beautiful stained glass window the National Trust presented to him in 1991. If it were ever fair to generalize about any group of people, Sybil's calm warmth and steady keenness would serve as a fine example of the Cayman character. In addition to running an impeccably ordered household with deceptively little effort, she owns a small store in Savannah of diverse island-made crafts and clothing. Sybil is thinking about a new name for her store, and laments that Children's Corner gets mistaken too often for a daycare center.

As we regretfully wind down our visit, Otto has already gone back to tend the cattle, and Sybil comes out to hug us good-bye with a container of freshly cut mango, crackers, a jar of their own honey and mango jam, forks and wet wipes for the road. It's not difficult to imagine returning and resuming our friendship sometime in the future. 🌸

LEFT: Horse near Castle Road, where the welcome sight of farmland still abounds.

OPPOSITE: In Bodden Town, a southwestern exposure necessitates slatted shutters.

PAGE 71: Ripe mangoes dangle from a branch in Otto Watler's grove.

PAGE 70: A macaw raised as a permanent pet. Mr. Watler, by contrast, has raised several Caymanian parrots in captivity to be successfully relased into their natural habitat. These parrots mature in three to four years, and then mate for life.

Banana leaf

"It gives me such pleasure, why shouldn't I let you in?"

response to being thanked for hospitality

Living Life Cayman Style

RIGHT: Buoys hang from a tree to designate fishermen's favorite spot in East End.

OPPOSITE: Dock on the north side

A pair of silver tree frogs.

ABOVE: Waves crash dramatically on the shores in West Bay

OPPOSITE LEFT: "Out-ray-jus" berthed at the Cayman Islands Yacht Club.

OPPOSITE RIGHT: A peaceful finish to the day's activities.

A species of Plumeria, commonly known as frangipani

ABOVE: A white picket fence lends an air of quaintness to this Boggy Sand Road house.

OPPOSITE: Beautifully landscaped sand garden on Boggy Sand Road

Living Life Cayman Style

Living Life Cayman Style

Pirates Week

Since 1976, the last week of October has marked the Pirate's Week National Festival. At that time, the Cayman Islands hark back to the days of pirate invasions, complete with fireworks, parades, and a week-long series of Heritage Days. Each community (Bodden Town, East End, George Town, North Side, Savannah-Newlands, and West Bay) has a designated day for a street fair and cultural display, which serves to highlight their unique features and showcases local crafts, artifacts, and cuisine.

Pirate's Week attracts tourists from around the world, including the infamous Seattle Seafair pirates. This motley crew is known for their orchestration of the staged "takeover" of George Town, where scores of pirates and wenches in colorful attire "seize" the governor and the town explodes in a festival atmosphere of parades, music, and merriment. This event kicks off the week's festivities, which end on October 31 at midnight, when the rowdy pirates are banished until the following October.

The colorful costumes, water and road races, children's activities, and song and dance fests make this week special. To visit Cayman during Pirate's Week is to be given the opportunity to go back in time, to learn about Cayman as it once was, and to experience the excitement of Cayman as it is today. ♥

LEFT: The Seattle Seafair Pirates

ABOVE: Two women sit and chat with vistors in the traditional Caymanian house on display during West Bay Heritage Day.

OPPOSITE RIGHT: A West Bay Heritage Day volunteer demonstrates how to prepare a coconut.

PAGE 80: Barbecue's hot and tasty on the street in George Town.

*"Don't break your camera on
me, child."*

a common response to being photographed

ABOVE: A young patriot assumes the face of the Cayman mascot, the sea turtle.

RIGHT: A brilliant variety of the Canna species

OPPOSITE: A festive float participant sprays the crowd with confetti.

Earl

Tomlinson

artist

Earl Tomlinson's brightly-painted gift shop is across the street from the Portofino wreck site. The day we met him, he was in the shade of his shop's covered front porch, painting coconut shells to sell along with the other island crafts he markets. He was using a color chart, and he was able to produce identical coconut carvings of parrots with amazing accuracy. We asked him if he minded the lack of customers, as it was summer and not tourist season. He laughed and shook his head. "I like the slow season. It gives me time to think."

899

Christmas in Cayman

Christmastime has historically been a highlight of the year for Caymanians. Sand is "backed" (starting as early as October, sand is obtained from the beach and brought home via basket, bucket, or wheelbarrow) and deposited in the front yard, where the fresh layer is painstakingly raked out over the existing sand and edged with pink conch shells. Residents often put a fresh coat of paint on their houses so that everything looks nice for Christmas. In more recent years some people have added impressive displays of yuletide lights. Among the many transformed yards stands the Crighton family's display, with its towering strands of bulbs illuminating every tree and multiple displays featuring the Nativity, Santa Claus, Disney characters, and even a quaint replica of an early Caymanian cottage decorated for a traditional Christmas. 🐚

OPPOSITE: A ship in George Town harbor is decked out with strings of lights for Christmas.

RIGHT: Church of God in West Bay.

ABOVE: Nativity scene at the Crighton home. Approximately a dozen scenes, some animated and some traditional, decorate every inch of their yard.

RIGHT: In the days of fewer inhabitants, residents would take a sage broom and rake a fresh layer of sand over their sand yards. The story goes that if one footprint made its way onto the pristine surface, the owner of the print could always be identified.

OPPOSITE: The Crighton family share Christmas cheer by this fantastic display in excess of thirty thousand lights, which grows every year.

Sister Islands

Solitude, Twice Removed

Approximately eighty-nine miles off the north-eastern end of Grand Cayman are the islands dubbed the Sister Islands, Cayman Brac and Little Cayman. Supposedly, these two islands were spotted by Columbus before he sighted Grand Cayman. They, and the waters surrounding them, were populated by multitudes of turtles, inspiring Columbus to dub them "Los Tortugas (The Turtles). A trip to the Sister Islands provides a glimpse into the Cayman of the past. As unhurried as Grand Cayman is, imagine taking that down a notch or two and there you have the pace of life on the Sister Islands. As new travelers to the sister islands, we also noticed the startling brilliance and clarity of the water and sky. To those fortunate travelers who reach their shores, the Sister Islands offer true solitude and unique natural beauty, both above and below the surface of their crystal clear waters.

Little Cayman

Little Cayman was commercialized, if you can call it that, ten years ago when the first and only store was built a short jog from the airport hut. Ten miles long and less than two miles across at its widest point, Little Cayman seems to exist in its own dimension. While a low-pressure system hovers one day over the main island, Little Cayman skies remain intensely blue all day. But more to the point, its slower pace and miniscule population, currently 107, with barely a handful of low-key resorts for visitors, ensure that this small paradise remains just that.

Little Cayman is so small that it often posesses only one example of something: one store stocks food staples and fishing tackle, one full-service restaurant provides a comfortable gathering place, one policeman maintains law and order, and one place of worship, the Little Cayman Baptist Church, opens its doors to everyone on the island, regardless of religion. Without

ABOVE: A storm-damaged dock remains at Sandy Point.

OPPOSITE ABOVE: View of Jackson's Pond

OPPOSITE BELOW: Point of Sand, or Sandy Point, at East End

a school on the island, the current pastor and his wife home-school their thirteen-year-old and sixteen-year-old, the only school-age children living on Little Cayman.

Before starting our jaunt, McLaughlin's Jeep Rental instructs us to leave the keys in the ignition at all times because while theft is not a part of the island's

vocabulary, keys lost in the sand are. In keeping with the theme of oneness, in our two-and-a-half-hour tour of the island's perimeter we pass one vehicle and one iguana loping across the road. Regularly posted signs warn drivers to drive slowly and to watch out for iguanas, which on most days shuffle onto the road with some frequency. About forty minutes into our drive, the pavement gives

way to a sandy dirt road, which continues for most of the way around the island. At the east end of the island, we find perhaps the most dramatic landscape at Point of Sand, a.k.a. Sandy Point, where cross currents head toward a shore of fine white sand heavily flecked with paprika-colored grains. The only movement comes from the wind pushing a steady ripple of crystal clear water onto the expanse of empty beach.

Around the bend, the climate becomes distinctly more arid, and large, succulent plants, laden with armies of butterflies, suddenly appear amidst the tropical brush. Out here, the highest point on the island looms at a scant forty feet, while the interior majority is filled with brackish water that attracts a variety of birds, including the endangered red-footed booby.

Upon our return to the starting point, we overhear one friend greeting another as they sit

RIGHT: If things are not maintained on Little Cayman, nature takes over.

OPPOSITE TOP: A deserted beach, Preston Bay

OPPOSITE MIDDLE: Bindweed, also known as seaside morning glory creeps onto beaches, where it takes hold in the sand with its unusually long roots.

OPPOSITE BOTTOM: Traditional-style accommodations at Paradise Villas

down to their regular lunch date at the Hungry Iguana Restaurant, a comfortable, high-ceilinged establishment built of red cedar. "Same time, same place—that's Little Cayman," she confirms. The most prominently displayed paper on the restaurant's community board is the National Weather Bureau's daily report. Conspicuously lacking is the usual collage of business cards. After all, unless you own a fishing boat or a dive business, there's not much reason to advertise here in this oasis of solitude. 🐚

A prudent speed limit helps protect the large number
of iguanas inhabiting the island.

ABOVE: Near West End Point

OPPOSITE TOP: Aerial view of the south side of the island

OPPOSITE BOTTOM: The island's airport and fire station exude anything
but a sense of formality.

OPPOSITE LEFT: The Little Cayman Museum, which stands next to the
Baptist Church, and is run by the pastor's wife.

Joel
Robert
Johnson
contract
plumber

We met Mr. Johnson on a return flight to Grand Cayman from Cayman Brac. We had stopped in Little Cayman to pick him up, along with several other passengers. He had just put in a full day of work and was happy to be heading home to Bodden Town. He loves the solitude and tranquility of Little Cayman. "Little Cayman is as Cayman was," he told us.

Cayman Brac

Cayman Brac is separated from Little Cayman by approximately seven miles of ocean. Of the two Sister Islands, Cayman Brac is the larger one, measuring twelve miles long and just over a mile wide. Currently, it is home to around 2,000 close-knit, friendly souls.

Cayman Brac's most prominent geographical feature is the rocky bluff ("Brac" is Gaelic for bluff) which rises dramatically up from sea level to a height of 140 feet, covering a good portion of the midsection of the island. The Brac has played an important role in the island's history. Back in 1932, a catastrophic hurricane swept the island and 109 people were killed. The 400 inhabitants who survived this disaster did so by seeking refuge in the caves which burrow into the Brac.

With characteristic fortitude, the island

RIGHT: Meandering path to the beach at Spot Bay
OPPOSITE LEFT: View of the Brac from Spot Bay
OPPOSITE RIGHT: A steeple bell at the historic West End Baptist Church on Cayman Brac.

recovered from the "Storm of '32" and now appears so idyllically tranquil that a tragedy of that magnitude occurring on these sleepy, sunny shores seems unthinkable. We land at the Gerrard Smith Airport, located on the western end of the island near a town named, appropriately, West End. After renting a car, we're off, traversing the north side of the island from west to east. On the road we pass many quiet streets with colorful, modest homes. Laundry hangs on clotheslines, drying in the tropical breeze. Chickens, dogs, and the occasional horse or cow populate the yards. To our north is the coral beach and ocean, and to our south, the dramatic starkness of the Brac. We stop to investigate a grand, slightly faded structure, with "E.A. Carter" written in peeling black painted letters atop the façade. This was once a store which supplied the island with food, dry goods, and medicine.

We then pay a visit to the Cayman Brac Museum, which is housed in what was originally the post office. Inside, there is an impressive selection of artifacts and memorabilia, including information on the seafaring industry, the hurricane of '32, and the controlled sinking of the Russian frigate, the *Captain Keith Tibbetts*, in 1996. (This submerged vessel provides a diversely populated, lively dive site.)

To find out even more about the island, we decide to investigate some of the caves, eighteen of which pepper the brac. Some of these caves, which contain several chambers and interesting stalagmites and stalactites, are quite large and can easily fit a crowd of tourists, while other caves are so tiny that an intrepid adventurer would be forced to crawl through alone on hands and knees. Often, accessing these caves requires sturdy walking shoes and a degree of determination. One of our photographers

lion lizard

climbed up to Peter's Cave and was rewarded with a magnificent view of Spot Bay. He was also greatly surprised to see eight cows munching on the lush vegetation atop the Brac.

Cayman Brac's unique topography sets it apart from the other two Cayman Islands. The rocky bluff and its surrounding thick vegetation evokes the feeling of a tropical rain forest.

Indigenous wildlife includes butterflies, bats, and the endangered Cayman Brac parrot (check out the 180-acre parrot reserve located atop the bluff). This island, from its meandering caves to its varied dive sites, is fascinating to explore, and its beauty, while not gentle, is ruggedly dramatic.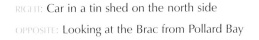

RIGHT: Car in a tin shed on the north side
OPPOSITE: Looking at the Brac from Pollard Bay

Reverend

C. Russell

Turner, Jr.

Baptist minister

& missionary

Tuesday morning, off season, small island in the Caribbean. There we are, the three of us, crammed into a rental jeep and driving down a rutted, barely traveled road on the quiet island of Cayman Brac. We pull the car over because one of us has spotted an intriguing footpath, and the consensus is that it likely leads to the beach. The three of us emerge from the car and walk down this path, through the dense vegetation and over bits of rock and coral, until we come to an opening. Indeed, it is the beach, but not a smooth, sandy one. This beach slopes down to the water and is covered with chunks of coral. A man approaches. He is tall, dressed head to toe on this sweltering day in a flannel shirt, long pants, boots, gloves, and a brimmed hat. He clutches a walking stick firmly in his hand. We are stunned to see another human being, let alone a man who looks as if he'd be more at home on the shores of Maine. On the other hand, he doesn't look one bit surprised to see us.

He greets us warmly. We explain that we're here to take pictures for a book we're working on, and he seems genuinely interested. He tells us that he's a pastor at the nearby Baptist church and that he has lived on the island for thirty years. During that time, he and his wife happily raised their five children. "We were only supposed to stay a year, but we just never wanted to leave." Noticing our glances at his attire, he explains that he is supposed to keep his skin protected from the sun's rays and that he walks the beach almost every day for exercise. Reaching into his pocket for his wallet, he pulls out exactly three religious tracts. His wallet contains no more, no less. He hands us each one. We thank him for his time, and we tell him that we hope our paths will cross again someday. Then, he starts to turn to continue his walk on the rocky beach.

"You know," one of us says, "It's kind of strange, isn't it? I mean, how often do you meet people walking on this part of the beach?"

"Not often," he says. "This is a quiet spot. Not a tourist beach."

"But you didn't even seem surprised to see us."

He smiles. "Not in the least. God plans these things." He raises his walking stick in a final salute, and turns back down toward the water.

ABOVE: Stalactite inside one of the more spacious caverns, north side of the Brac

RIGHT BOTTOM: Mouth of the cave, north side

RIGHT TOP: A nocturnal bat sleeping as it hangs from a cavern ceiling

OPPOSITE: Trying its best to blend in, this snail is not quite invisible.

TOP: House in North East Bay

ABOVE: E. A. Carter homestead, which sits next to the oldest store building on Cayman Brac

LEFT: Near Cat Head Bay

OPPOSITE: Mango trees provide ample shade on an especially hot day.

Jewels of Interest

Queen Elizabeth II Botanic Park

The Queen Elizabeth II Botanic Park is a 65-acre area featuring native trees, plants, flowers, birds, reptiles, and butterflies. There is a Woodland Trail, which meanders through the park and is lined with indigenous vegetation, as well as the Garden of Flowering Plants, which contains two and a half acres of floral gardens arranged by color.

You can also glimpse into Cayman history when you visit the Heritage Garden. A sand path lined with conch shells leads to a traditional Caymanian house. This house was relocated from East End, where it had originally housed a family of eleven. Surrounding the house is a sand yard dotted with fruit trees and plants, such as plantains, cassava, and sweet potato, and medicinal plants such as aloe vera, which would have been planted around a Caymanian house a century ago.

The park offers a place to learn more about the flora, fauna, and history of Cayman, or, for those less ambitious visitors, a place to stroll, relax, and contemplate the beauty of this island.

ABOVE: View of the blue pergola topped with skyflower at Queen Elizabeth II Botanic Park. Behind the structure stand two travelers' trees, a distant relative of the banana tree, and on the left a blue latan palm adds texture to the scene.

OPPOSITE TOP: Thunbergia grandiflora, or skyflower

OPPOSITE FAR RIGHT: Alpinia purpurata, or Ginger lily in all its splendor

PREVIOUS PAGE: A traditional dwelling and sand yard at the Botanic Park

CHAPTER OPENER: A Monet-like water lily at the Queen Elizabeth II Botanic Park

Succulent along the Wooded Trail

Mrs. E. W.
Whittaker
"Miss Winnie"
retired
schoolteacher

At the end of a quiet lane off a busy street in George Town is a small cottage with a shady front porch, flowering hibiscus in the yard, and an occasional chicken strolling across the path. This is the quiet, comfortable home of Miss Winnie. When we arrive to talk to her, she ushers us in politely but briskly and tells us to have a seat. "This is my favorite soap opera. It will be over in three minutes." She is right. When the final credits begin to roll, she switches the television off and settles back onto the sofa, ready to talk. Miss Winnie is not a frivolous woman. There is nothing casual or off-hand about the interview. Miss Winnie has clearly thought about everything we discuss, and has formed definite opinions, which she enjoys sharing.

Miss Winnie grew up on a farm in West Bay. Her father, James Alexander Evans, grew a variety of fruits and vegetables. "God never made a more wonderful man," she tells us, recalling how he grew an abundance of produce, which he always shared with their neighbors. "My father was generous, kind, and never too busy to listen. His memory is sweet to me." Miss Winnie loved her mother, too—"she was a good, hard-working mother"—but felt that she was always too busy to take time from nursing and attending to the needs of others to enjoy her children. "She kept herself so busy that she was never able to slow down." Miss Winnie learned from this. When she married and raised her two sons, she sacrificed to make the time to be with them. "I don't just mean doing my work. I mean, helping them with their homework, playing games with them." She also believes in not sparing the rod. "Discipline. But only discipline when you aren't really mad. Then you don't lash out in anger. That is the worst thing for a child." The best thing for a child? "Unconditional love." A tribute to the efficacy of her child-rearing efforts is the fact that her two grown sons are educated, happy, and successful. Both live on Cayman and visit frequently.

Miss Winnie talks at length about her childhood. She remembers "getting together to eat popcorn. When the mosquitoes got too bad, we'd stay indoors and study the Bible. There was a lot of laughter in our homes. We'd play games and sing songs and have family time. Then, everyone got together at church." Christmastime provides the most vivid memories for Miss Winnie. She remembers people going to the beach with thatch baskets and wheelbarrows to collect fresh sand, which was "backed" (carried) to the front yards so that a clean layer could be raked over the existing sand, "which gave the appearance of fresh snow." Gifts were simple. "We had stockings filled with homemade gifts and peppermints. Everyone was happy with what little they got."

Our favorite story of the several Miss Winnie tells involves one of her devoutly Christian neighbors, who believed in keeping the Sabbath. Everyone in the neighborhood worked hard on Saturday to prepare for their day of rest, but this woman was even more zealous than most. She woke up one Sunday, though, only to realize with dismay that she had forgotten to pick the breadfruit she had noticed hanging on a tree in her yard the day before. After much deliberation, she dashed outside and seized the breadfruit, then told her neighbors that "I think I picked it so fast that God did

not see me." Miss Winnie's eyes twinkles as she tells that story.

When we leave Miss Winnie, she walks us outside into her front yard, which is vibrant with hibiscus, roses, and snow-on-the-mountain. While office and apartment buildings rise up all around, Miss Winnie's yard is an oasis of tranquility. Change is inevitable, but Miss Winnie resolutely holds on to her piece of old Cayman.

Stingray City

This is one of the most remarkable things to do when visiting Cayman. From a protected area of shallow, crystal-clear water in the north sound, which you can reach by sailboat, motorboat, or catamaran, you can swim alongside, or simply watch scores of stingrays. These gentle creatures are amazing to watch and touch—they glide effortlessly through the water, and their skin feels smooth and soft as chamois. For years tourists have been allowed to feed the stingrays, but are now discouraged from this practice, so that the stingrays don't become dependent on humans. It is a wholly unique experience to be in the water with these elegant creatures, as they brush past, unafraid of their human visitors. 🐚

ABOVE: Aboard a catamaran, all geared up for an excursion into the waters of Stingray City

OPPOSITE RIGHT: Shots like this "half and half" photo taken at Stingray City are among the most difficult in underwater photography.

OPPOSITE LEFT: One of the photographers takes a break as he allows a stingray to rest gently underwater on his hands. Lifting these creatures out of the water is now discouraged.

Hell

After spending your days gazing at serene blue waters, gently swaying palm trees, and graceful sloped pale sand beaches, this sooty, ragged outcrop of ironshore provides a visual shock by contrast. Welcome to Hell, Grand Cayman, where visitors can stand on a simple wooden deck while they survey the decidedly inhospitable environment, made up of craggy ironshore coral coated by dark microorganisms which provide the charred look of the underworld. There are two fun-to-browse-through gift shops here, where one can purchase a variety of Hell-inspired paraphernalia, as well as a post office where you can send mail postmarked from Hell.

ABOVE: Ironshore coral holds rainwater in Hell.

Gladwyn
K. Bush
"Miss Lassie"
intuitive artist

While working on this book, we went to visit Miss Lassie twice. On our first visit, no one appeared to be home. However, the door was wide open, and as Miss Lassie doesn't own a car, we later surmised that she was in her bedroom, catching a late morning nap. On our second visit, we yell through the open door a bit louder, and a slender, silver-haired woman shuffles to the door in her stocking feet. She greets us—two complete strangers!—with a radiant smile, and without a moment's hesitation invites us into her colorful, cluttered living room.

Miss Lassie is a blend of gentle calm and unbounded energy. She has just completed a painting commissioned by the Mormon Church in Utah, and it is perched on her sofa, ready to be shipped off. She graciously offers us chairs to sit on in her front parlor, which overflows with her paintings on canvasses, cushions, walls, shutters, and doorframes. Miss Lassie's closest companion is her dog, Comfort, an affable Shepherd mix who seems to love nothing more than burying his head in visitors' laps.

Miss Lassie is the youngest of eleven children, with eight brothers and two sisters. Her great-great-grandfather was the first white settler on Grand Cayman. As is the case with many Caymanians, Miss Lassie is descended from a white man and a slave. Miss Lassie adored her father and freely admits to being the pet of the family. Her brothers would occasionally tease her, and their punishment was rocking her for hours on the hammock on her front porch. Miss Lassie married Charles Christopher Bush, a seaman who served on eleven ships from 1939 to 1945. Upon returning to Cayman after his last voyage, Miss Lassie says, "he was not in his right mind." "He would have spells," Miss Lassie tells us. "I took care of him, though. Me and my son walked with him as he walked." When we express to her how difficult this must have been, she smiles and shrugs. "You grows used to something you don't bring on yourself."

Miss Lassie used to draw in school as a child but didn't start painting in earnest until she was sixty-two. Then, one day she had a divine inspiration when she was half-awake, and she seized the only avail-

able paint in her house—standard house paint—and began to render her vision on the top and bottom halves of her front door. Once she started painting from these inspirations, there was no stopping her. From her first painting, she progressed to painting her doors and walls, then objects like throw pillows and refrigerators (we saw several of these festively decorated appliances), then her ceilings, outbuildings, and any other surface that lent itself to pigment and brush. It was not until many years into the creation of her paintings, or "markings," as she likes to call them, that she was introduced to oil paints and canvas. Most of her work is derived from the Bible. She feels called upon to paint, and it is from that calling, and her love of composing and playing music, that she feels joy and a sense of purpose.

Miss Lassie knows she'll see Jesus someday. However, she is not ready to go anytime soon. "I am still too full of sin," she laughs. "But when I go, I know I'll walk through the Valley with a fearless tread." Her main sorrow is that she rarely sees her son. "He is too fond of the rum," she tells us, shaking her head. Still, the money she has made from her paintings, which is fairly considerable, she keeps in the bank for her son. She has chosen to live the same as she always has, cozy in her childhood home, surrounded by a familiar jumble of artifacts. She throws nothing away. We see evidence of this fact as we follow her, in her stocking feet, around her property. Old conch shells, tires, plastic bottles, a decrepit rowboat. . .we are, at all times, surrounded by the accumulated detritus of a lifetime. She takes us through her guest house and shows us the window that an intruder had smashed in an effort to break in. This violation had shaken her, and she speaks sadly of the increase in crime on the island. Shortly, though, she brightens and offers us something cool to drink from one of her operative refrigerators, which is fully stocked with Coke, Diet Coke, and Sprite. We listen to her play on her keyboard a hymn she has composed, her voice clear and full of feeling. When we thank her for her willingness to open her heart and home to us, she looks genuinely bewildered. "It gives me such pleasure, why shouldn't I let you in? I thank you for your kindness." When we leave, we truly feel that we have been touched by this extraordinary woman, who has steadfastly followed her calling, and by doing so, uncovered her purpose in life.

Rum Point

Rum Point is a shaded, tranquil spot, marked by giant casuarinas with hammocks, for ultimate relaxation, draped between them. You can rent a windsurfer, wave runner, or snorkeling equipment, or do what most visitors to this quiet spot do—absolutely nothing. Rum Point's name is derived from a shipwreck years ago in which barrels of rum were washed ashore. You can reach Rum Point either by car, or by the Rum Point ferry, which leaves from the Hyatt Hotel Marina.

ABOVE: These are the only posted guidelines to enjoying your stay at Rum Point.

RIGHT: The ferry to Rum Point

OPPOSITE LEFT: Rum Point ferry dock

OPPOSITE FAR LEFT: View north from Rum Point

"I was drawn to the people.
They are intellectual and
God-fearing."

resident of Savannah, Grand Cayman

ABOVE: Last light at the Royal Palms Beach Club

OPPOSITE: A couple enjoys a romantic dinner at the Grand Old House.

The Turtle Farm

The Turtle Farm in West Bay is an amazing spot, home to roughly sixteen thousand turtles. The majority of these reptilian residents are green sea turtles, which get their name from the green hue of the fat deposits under the skin. The farm looks rather like a large outdoor science lab, complete with holding tanks, inset pools, and conduits for the turtles to navigate. From a humble beginning in 1968 in the community of Salt Creek,

ABOVE: This green sea turtle looks up as if to see what all the fuss is about.

LEFT: A group of tourists gather around the holding tank at the turtle farm.

where the turtles were originally raised for their meat, leather, and oil products, the Turtle Farm was relocated in 1971 to its present site, where the turtles were fed a new, more nutritious diet, and, since 1980, twenty-nine thousand green sea turtles have been tagged and released into the wild. This number is especially significant, as green sea turtles are on the endangered species list. The Turtle Farm does not collect eggs or turtles from the wild. It is the only totally self-sufficient turtle ranch in the world. One note—roughly fifty turtles per month from the secondary turtle herd are harvested each month, and the meat is sold locally. You can even try turtle soup or turtle sandwiches in the Turtle Farm cafeteria. The Turtle Farm offers a unique glimpse into both Cayman's past, when turtles were a large part of the Caymanian diet, and Cayman's future, which places a high premium on protecting the environment and endangered wildlife. Come ready to hold a turtle or two, and watch some of the adult turtles, weighing between 200 and 650 pounds, swim gracefully through the water. It's an experience you won't forget. 🐚

RIGHT: This young turtle would rather be swimming.

OPPOSITE: Smiles, ahoy! The *Jolly Roger* sets sail at twilight.

RIGHT: The light emanating from the restaurant, Lighthouse at Breakers, was at one time so blinding that it caused navigational problems for seafarers. Eventually the light source was blocked.
BELOW: The blowhole at East End

Marigolds at the Botanic Park

Pedro St. James, or Pedro's Castle

Pedro St. James, also known locally as Pedro's Castle, enjoys an enchanting setting on one of the very few elevated coastal spots on the island of Grand Cayman. The lush green grounds are beautifully landscaped with scenic walkways and a variety of flowers, shrubs, and palm trees, all of which ends sharply at the craggy cliff face, which drops

dramatically into the azure waters below. Pedro's Castle is the oldest building on Cayman. It was built in 1780 by William Eden, who had arrived on Cayman from England. Pedro St. James's foundation and supporting walls are made up of thick stone, which give the interior both strength and coolness. Pedro St. James swiftly became the most important structure on the island, and it served as a courthouse, a jail, and a community refuge in the nineteenth century. Then, in 1877, lightning struck, killing Mary Jane Eden, the daughter of the owner at the time, Joseph Eden. The house was abandoned immediately thereafter, since members of the Eden family considered it bad luck.

Over the next seventy years, Pedro St. James was left to the elements. Hurricanes and time battered the structure, but still, the stone walls stood. Finally, it was bought by an American entrepreneur named Thomas Hubbell, who renovated it to make it look more like a castle, complete with battlements. He billed it as a pirate's lair, and it swiftly became a tourist attraction. Years later, Hubbell leased it as a hotel and restaurant. After fires swept the building on several occasions, the government bought Pedro St.

James in 1991 and restored it to its 1780 appearance. It was opened to the public in 1998 and now offers a state-of-the-art theater which features a multimedia show telling the history of this lovely plantation home. There is a gift shop, restaurant, and a friendly and knowledgeable staff of docents to show you about the house and grounds. 🐚

LEFT & ABOVE: George Town's harbor has been port to many vessels, old and new.

OPPOSITE LEFT: The center of George Town—you can get anywhere from here now, as opposed to decades ago when the lack of roads in some parts of the island prevented some inhabitants from ever visiting other parts of the island.

OPPOSITE BELOW: This buccaneer stands watch outside one of Grand Cayman's main bookstores, the Book Nook.

OPPOSITE RIGHT: The Cayman Islands National Museum is home to Cayman's most treasured artifacts.

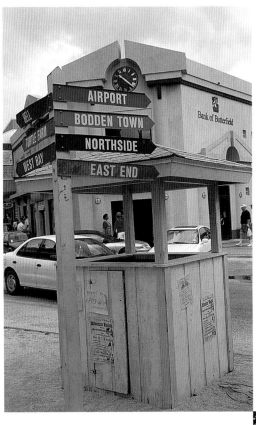

"I recall a time when there were more churches than banks on Cayman."

eighth-generation Caymanian

ABOVE: Ixora, or flame-of-the-forest

OPPOSITE: Ristorante Pappagallo, one of Cayman's finest restaurants

Hope

Ebanks

Glidden

& her daughter

Hope

Glidden

Stephenson

Hope Glidden Borden, Sister Hope to some, Miss Hopie or Miss Hope to seemingly everyone else on Cayman, is a force. Her grin is infectious, her laugh, from the heart, and her inner warmth draw you in and hold you close. Hope has an enormous following. When she had emergency surgery last year, the doctors were overwhelmed by the size and tenacity of her fan club. They finally had to insist on no calls or visitors so that she was able to find the quiet she needed to recover. From that bout with illness, she has rallied one hundred percent, and the only reminder of her hospitalization is an enormous scrapbook, which contains only a portion of the numerous cards from loving friends, family, and acquaintances.

Clearly, Hope is a woman who has touched many lives in a profound way. She is seventy-three and shows no sign of slowing down. She joined the Cayman Islands Civil Service as a clerk typist before her eighteenth birthday, and when she retired on December 31, 1976, she had risen to the position of postmaster general of the Cayman Islands, the first woman in Cayman's history to hold this post. For the past twelve years she has been employed by Cayman Airways, the national flag carrier of the Cayman Islands, as an executive secretary, and more recently, she competently handles the duties of head receptionist. Hope is also one of the speakers on the weekly radio broadcast of her church, the Church of God (Universal), and her volunteer work includes playing piano and organ at her own church and at other churches for weddings, funerals, and other special functions. All told, she is in a state of constant motion.

Her daughter, Hope Stephenson, or "Pie" to her friends and family, is, like her mother, never idle. Hers is the first face you see when you enter the impressive glass foyer of the main government building, or the Glass House, as it is called on Cayman. Hope is a bit more sedate than her mother. Her smile is more delicate, and her laugh is gentler, but Pie has inherited every bit of her mother's warmth and generosity of spirit. It seems quite fitting that both Hopes should greet people at important entrances to Cayman. It is almost as if they are the Caymans incarnate—beautiful, warm, sunny, industrious, but always giving the sense that they have unlimited time for you.

Mother Hope is a sixth-generation Caymanian, one of six children born to a minister of the Church of God in West Bay. She and her siblings were all born at home in West Bay. Hope still lives in her childhood home, and although there have been certain improvements (the addition of a front hallway and door, and the convenience of modern plumbing), much of the house is unchanged. She married, only to have her husband desert her during the time of her pregnancy. The reason? He was at sea at the time and heard rumors, started by her jealous in-laws "who never thought much" of her, that she was running around with other men. To her enormous credit, Hope never passed down to Pie any bitterness as a result of this abandonment. "There was no chip on my shoulder. I just said my prayers and carried on. I had a child to raise." When Pie was born, she was surrounded by love from aunts, cousins, and friends. Eventually, Pie did get to know her father, whom she adored. Mother Hope now lives with her sister-in-law, Pat, and they are remarkably supportive of one another and admirably self-sufficient. Their home is comfortable, organized and tidy, but full of memorabilia from lives fully lived.

From her seat behind the high front desk at the Glass House, Pie greets everyone, from the delivery men to the Governor himself, with the same kind smile and conscientious deference. She is married to Hamlin Stephenson, a handsome man from Jamaica whom she first spotted at a church picnic when she was a teenager. Hamlin is, by trade, a very successful builder, but his heart is in his sideline—farming and raising goats. Pie and Hamlin have a modest-sized farm in Savannah. During one visit, Hamlin and Pie talked about the challenges of raising livestock, from the early-morning crowing of the roosters to the occasional stray dog that tries to infiltrate their property and snatch their goats.

Pie is an excellent cook, and she introduced us to heavy cake, a dessert prepared with sweet potatoes or cassava (both roots, finely ground)and lots of sugar and spices. The weight of this confection is astounding, as is its uniquely thick, rather gelatinous texture, but it's delicious. Pie told us about how heavy cake determined the traditional Caymanian's weekend. When you ask if someone had a good weekend, they are apt to reply, "Yes, it was good, I had some heavy cake." A bad weekend meant no heavy cake.

Mother Hope and Pie have a beautiful relationship, based on mutual love and respect. Seeing them together, laughing, holding hands, so connected, is a wonderful thing. Pie and Hamlin's relationship draws on this fundamental bond—the same respect, humor, and caring is there, too. Both Hopes recall with some sadness, "when there were more churches than banks on Cayman." They fear the new affluence that has come to Cayman will spark acquisitiveness and greed. However, they are in contact with a number of young people who are firmly "church-centered," as Pie expresses it, and their thoughts for Cayman's future are guardedly optimistic.

Mother Hope and Pie are traditional Caymanian women. This is not to say that they are old-fashioned. The tradition they embody is that of strong, independent women, accepting of hardship but equal to the task of taking on life's battles with humor, grace, and humility. 🌸

ABOVE: A native feast, including fruit from the gourd tree, passion fruit, avocado, calamondin oranges, sour sop, akee, and star fruit, decorates a display at Savannah-Newlands Heritage Day.

OPPOSITE: The George Town Post Office, where Hope Glidden served for many years as the first postmistress general.

FOLLOWING PAGE: George Town silhouetted at the onset of evening.

Photo Credits